MW00973147

To

Jason & Danielle

From

Dwayne, Jessica, Karlee & Braxton

Now these three remain:
faith, hope, and love.
But the greatest of these is love.

—

1 Corinthians 13:13 HCSB

Love Is...
Forever

Freeman-Smith, a division of Worthy Media, Inc.
134 Franklin Road, Suite 200, Brentwood, Tennessee 37027

The quoted ideas expressed in this book (but not Scripture verses) are not, in all cases, exact quotations, as some have been edited for clarity and brevity. In all cases, the author has attempted to maintain the speaker's original intent. In some cases, quoted material for this book was obtained from secondary sources, primarily print media. While every effort was made to ensure the accuracy of these sources, the accuracy cannot be guaranteed. For additions, deletions, corrections, or clarifications in future editions of this text, please write Freeman-Smith.

Scripture quotations are taken from:

The Holy Bible, King James Version

The Holy Bible, New International Version (NIV) Copyright © 1973, 1978, 1984, by International Bible Society. Used by permission of Zondervan Publishing House. All rights reserved.

The New American Standard Bible®, (NASB) Copyright © 1960, 1962, 1963, 1968, 1971, 1972, 1973, 1975, 1977, 1995 by The Lockman Foundation. Used by permission.

The Holy Bible, New King James Version (NKJV) Copyright © 1982 by Thomas Nelson, Inc. Used by permission.

The Holy Bible, New Living Translation, (NLT) Copyright © 1996. Used by permission of Tyndale House Publishers, Inc., Wheaton, Illinois 60189. All rights reserved.

New Century Version®. (NCV) Copyright © 1987, 1988, 1991 by Word Publishing, a division of Thomas Nelson, Inc. All rights reserved. Used by permission.

The Message (MSG) This edition issued by contractual arrangement with NavPress, a division of The Navigators, U.S.A. Originally published by NavPress in English as THE MESSAGE: The Bible in Contemporary Language copyright 2002-2003 by Eugene Peterson. All rights reserved.

International Children's Bible®, New Century Version®. (ICB) Copyright © 1986, 1988, 1999 by Tommy Nelson™, a division of Thomas Nelson, Inc. All rights reserved. Used by permission.

The Holman Christian Standard Bible™ (HCSB) Copyright © 1999, 2000, 2001 by Holman Bible Publishers. Used by permission.

Cover Design by Kim Russell / Wahoo Designs
Page Layout by Bart Dawson

ISBN 978-1-60587-433-3

Printed in the United States of America

1 2 3 4 5—QGF—16 15 14 13 12

Love Is...
Forever

Introduction

"But the greatest of these is love"—seven familiar words that remind us of a simple truth: God places a high priority on love . . . and so should we. Faith is important, of course. So too is hope. But love is more important still.

Christ demonstrated His love for us on the cross, and, as Christians, we are called upon to return Christ's love by sharing it. We are commanded to love one another just as Christ loved us (John 13:34). That's a simple commandment to understand, but a difficult commandment to put into practice, especially when we're tired, frustrated, confused, or worried. But with Christ as our guide, we can demonstrate our love for others, even on those difficult days when we might prefer to do otherwise.

So do yourself (and your loved ones) a favor: take these ideas to heart and weave them into the fabric of your relationships. When you do, you'll learn firsthand the truth of God's Word: "the greatest of these" is now—and will forever be—love.

Chapter 1

Love Is . . .

Dear friends, if God loved us in this way,
we also must love one another.

—

1 John 4:11 HCSB

How do you define love? Is it simply a warm feeling that you feel in the pit of your stomach, or is it something more? Is it a fleeting burst of emotions that may be here today and gone tomorrow, or is it something more? Is love merely a strong physical attraction that you feel toward a person whose appearance you admire, or is it something more? If you answered "something more," you're right. Feelings of infatuation come and go, but genuine love isn't like that— real love lasts.

Genuine love is patient, understanding, consistent, and considerate. Genuine love doesn't just sit around and do nothing; it is translated into acts of kindness. Genuine love doesn't always spring up overnight, but it doesn't vanish overnight, either. And, genuine love requires effort. Simply put, if you wish to build lasting relationships, you must be willing to do your part.

God does not intend for you to experience mediocre relationships; He created you for far greater things. Building lasting relationships requires compassion, wisdom, empathy, kindness, courtesy, and forgiveness (lots of forgiveness). If that sounds a lot like work, it is—which is perfectly fine with God. Why? Because He knows that you are capable of doing that work, and because He knows that the fruits of your labors will enrich the lives of your loved ones and the lives of generations yet unborn.

Only joyous love redeems.

—

Catherine Marshall

If Jesus is the preeminent One in our lives, then we will love each other, submit to each other, and treat one another fairly in the Lord.

Warren Wiersbe

Those who abandon ship the first time it enters a storm miss the calm beyond. And the rougher the storms weathered together, the deeper and stronger real love grows.

Ruth Bell Graham

Love is an attribute of God. To love others is evidence of a genuine faith.

Kay Arthur

How do you spell love? When you reach the point where the happiness, security, and development of another person is as much of a driving force to you as your own happiness, security, and development, then you have a mature love. True love is spelled G-I-V-E. It is not based on what you can get, but rooted in what you can give to the other person.

Josh McDowell

12

Love must be supported and fed and protected, just like a little infant who is growing up at home.

James Dobson

Brotherly love is still the distinguishing badge of every true Christian.

Matthew Henry

Love is the seed of all hope. It is the enticement to trust, to risk, to try, and to go on.

Gloria Gaither

It is when we come to the Lord in our nothingness, our powerlessness and our helplessness that He then enables us to love in a way which, without Him, would be absolutely impossible.

Elisabeth Elliot

Love simply cannot spring up without that self-surrender to each other. If either withholds the self, love cannot exist.

E. Stanley Jones

I pray that you, being rooted and firmly established in love, may be able to comprehend with all the saints what is the breadth and width, height and depth, and to know the Messiah's love that surpasses knowledge, so you may be filled with all the fullness of God.

Ephesians 3:17-19 HCSB

If I speak the languages of men and of angels, but do not have love, I am a sounding gong or a clanging cymbal.

1 Corinthians 13:1 HCSB

Dear friends, if God loved us in this way, we also must love one another.

1 John 4:11 HCSB

And may the Lord cause you to increase and overflow with love for one another and for everyone, just as we also do for you.

1 Thessalonians 3:12 HCSB

14

Now the goal of our instruction is love from a pure heart, a good conscience, and a sincere faith.

1 Timothy 1:5 HCSB

Above all, put on love—the perfect bond of unity.

Colossians 3:14 HCSB

Love never gives up. Love cares more for others than for self. Love doesn't want what it doesn't have. Love doesn't strut, doesn't have a swelled head, doesn't force itself on others, Isn't always "me first," doesn't fly off the handle, doesn't keep score of the sins of others, doesn't revel when others grovel, takes pleasure in the flowering of truth, puts up with anything, trusts God always, always looks for the best, never looks back, but keeps going to the end.

1 Corinthians 13:4-7 MSG

We love because He first loved us.

1 John 4:19 HCSB

Love is not measured by
what it gets,
but by what it costs.

—

Oswald Chambers

Chapter 2

Sharing
God's Love

For the Lord is good, and His love is eternal;
His faithfulness endures through all generations.

—

Psalm 100:5 HCSB

Have you built your relationships on the solid foundation of God's love? Is God the foundation upon which you've built your marriage, your family, and your friendships? If so, you are wise, and you are blessed. If not, it's time to reconsider your priorities for life and for love.

God's love for you is deeper and more profound than you can fathom. And now, precisely because you are a wondrous creation treasured by God, a question presents itself: What will you do in response to God's love? Will you ignore it or embrace it? Will you return it or neglect it? The decision, of course, is yours and yours alone.

When you and your loved ones embrace God together, you are forever changed. When you embrace God's love, you will feel differently about yourself, your relationships, your family, and your world. When you embrace God's love together, you will share His message, and you will obey His commandments. When you do these things, your love will endure forever.

God is a God of unconditional, unremitting love, a love that corrects and chastens but never ceases.

Kay Arthur

"How can I give you up, Ephraim? How can I hand you over, Israel?" Substitute your own name for Ephraim and Israel. At the heart of the gospel is a God who deliberately surrenders to the wild, irresistible power of love.

Philip Yancey

As we stand at the Cross of Christ, we see a glorious exhibition of God's love.

Billy Graham

It is God to whom and with whom we travel, and while He is the End of our journey, He is also at every stopping place.

Elisabeth Elliot

God loves us the way we are, but He loves us too much to leave us that way.

Leighton Ford

The love of God is revealed in that He laid down His life for His enemies.

Oswald Chambers

Accepting God's love as a gift instead of trying to earn it had somehow seemed presumptuous and arrogant to me, when, in fact, my pride was tricking me into thinking that I could merit His love and forgiveness with my own strength.

Lisa Whelchel

As God's children, we are the recipients of lavish love—a love that motivates us to keep trusting even when we have no idea what God is doing.

Beth Moore

The great love of God is an ocean without a bottom or a shore.

C. H. Spurgeon

God loves each of us as if there were only one of us.

St. Augustine

Jesus loves us with fidelity, purity, constancy, and passion, no matter how imperfect we are.

Stormie Omartian

God's love is measureless. It is more: it is boundless. It has no bounds because it is not a thing but a facet of the essential nature of God. His love is something he is, and because he is infinite, that love can enfold the whole created world in itself and have room for ten thousand times ten thousand worlds beside.

A. W. Tozer

For God loved the world in this way: He gave His only Son, so that everyone who believes in Him will not perish but have eternal life.

John 3:16 HCSB

[Because of] the Lord's faithful love we do not perish, for His mercies never end. They are new every morning; great is Your faithfulness!

Lamentations 3:22-23 HCSB

Help me, Lord my God; save me according to Your faithful love.

Psalm 109:26 HCSB

Whoever is wise will observe these things, and they will understand the lovingkindness of the Lord.

Psalm 107:43 NKJV

Draw near to God, and He will draw near to you.

James 4:8 HCSB

The Lord is gracious and compassionate, slow to anger and great in faithful love. The Lord is good to everyone; His compassion [rests] on all He has made.

Psalm 145:8-9 HCSB

For He is gracious and compassionate, slow to anger, rich in faithful love.

Joel 2:13 HCSB

Praise the Lord, all you Gentiles! Laud Him, all you peoples! For His merciful kindness is great toward us, and the truth of the Lord endures forever. Praise the Lord!

Psalm 117:1-2 NKJV

Though we may not act like
our Father, there is
no greater truth than this:
We are his. Unalterably.
He loves us. Undyingly.
Nothing can separate us
from the love of Christ.

—

Max Lucado

Chapter 3

Love Is Kind

*Just as you want others to do for you,
do the same for them.*

—

Luke 6:31 HCSB

Never underestimate the power of kindness. You never know what kind word or gesture will significantly change someone's day, or week, or life.

Is your home like the Old West, a place "where never is heard a discouraging word and the skies are not cloudy all day" . . . or is the forecast at your house slightly cloudier than that? If your house is a place where the rule of the day is the Golden Rule, don't change a thing. Kindness starts at home, but it should never end there.

So today, slow yourself down and be alert for those who need your smile, your kind words, or your helping hand. Make kindness a centerpiece of your dealings with others. They will be blessed, and so will you.

If we have the true love of God in our hearts, we will show it in our lives. We will not have to go up and down the earth proclaiming it. We will show it in everything we say or do.

D. L. Moody

When we do little acts of kindness that make life more bearable for someone else, we are walking in love as the Bible commands us.

Barbara Johnson

A little kindly advice is better than a great deal of scolding.

Fanny Crosby

The mark of a Christian is that he will walk the second mile and turn the other cheek. A wise man or woman gives the extra effort, all for the glory of the Lord Jesus Christ.

John Maxwell

It is one of the most beautiful compensations of life that no one can sincerely try to help another without helping herself.

Barbara Johnson

When you extend hospitality to others, you're not trying to impress people, you're trying to reflect God to them.

Max Lucado

Do all the good you can. By all the means you can. In all the ways you can. In all the places you can. At all the times you can. To all the people you can. As long as ever you can.

John Wesley

Kindness in this world will do much to help others, not only to come into the light, but also to grow in grace day by day.

Fanny Crosby

Be so preoccupied with
good will that you
haven't room for ill will.

—

E. Stanley Jones

Finally, all of you be of one mind, having compassion for one another; love as brothers, be tenderhearted, be courteous.

1 Peter 3:8 NKJV

And may the Lord make you increase and abound in love to one another and to all.

1 Thessalonians 3:12 NKJV

And be kind and compassionate to one another, forgiving one another, just as God also forgave you in Christ.

Ephesians 4:32 HCSB

Pure and undefiled religion before our God and Father is this: to look after orphans and widows in their distress and to keep oneself unstained by the world.

James 1:27 HCSB

Love is patient; love is kind.

1 Corinthians 13:4 HCSB

Be hospitable to one another without complaining.

1 Peter 4:9 HCSB

Don't neglect to show hospitality, for by doing this some have welcomed angels as guests without knowing it.

Hebrews 13:2 HCSB

Carry one another's burdens; in this way you will fulfill the law of Christ.

Galatians 6:2 HCSB

When you launch
an act of kindness
out into the crosswinds of life,
it will blow kindness
back to you.

—

Dennis Swanberg

Chapter 4

Love Is Generous

He has dispersed abroad,
He has given to the poor;
His righteousness endures forever;
His horn will be exalted with honor.

—

Psalm 112:9 NKJV

God's Word promises that He rewards generosity. So if we sincerely desire to experience His greatest blessings, we must be generous with our time, our talents, our encouragement, and our possessions. When we become generous ambassadors for God, He blesses us in ways that we cannot fully understand. But if we allow ourselves to become closefisted and miserly, either with our possessions or with our love, we deprive ourselves of the spiritual abundance that would otherwise be ours.

Do you seek God's abundance and His peace? Then share the blessings that God has given you—and teach your family members to do likewise. God expects no less, and He deserves no less. And neither, come to think of it, do your neighbors.

We are never more like God than when we give.

Charles Swindoll

The measure of a life, after all, is not its duration but its donation.

Corrie ten Boom

The happiest and most joyful people are those who give money and serve.

Dave Ramsey

Abundant living means abundant giving.

E. Stanley Jones

God does not supply money to satisfy our every whim and desire. His promise is to meet our needs and provide an abundance so that we can help other people.

Larry Burkett

Here lies the tremendous mystery—that God should be all-powerful, yet refuse to coerce. He summons us to cooperation. We are honored in being given the opportunity to participate in His good deeds. Remember how He asked for help in performing His miracles: Fill the water pots, stretch out your hand, distribute the loaves.

Elisabeth Elliot

God does not need our money. But, you and I need the experience of giving it.

James Dobson

Let us give according to our incomes, lest God make our incomes match our gifts.

Peter Marshall

Two works of mercy set a man free: forgive and you will be forgiven, and give and you will receive.

St. Augustine

The mark of a Christian is that he will walk the second mile and turn the other cheek. A wise man or woman gives the extra effort, all for the glory of the Lord Jesus Christ.

John Maxwell

When somebody needs a helping hand, he doesn't need it tomorrow or the next day. He needs it now, and that's exactly when you should offer to help. Good deeds, if they are really good, happen sooner rather than later.

Marie T. Freeman

What is your focus today? Joy comes when it is Jesus first, others second . . . then you.

Kay Arthur

When it is in your power, don't withhold good from
the one to whom it is due.

Proverbs 3:27 HCSB

So whenever you give to the poor, don't sound a
trumpet before you, as the hypocrites do in the syna-
gogues and on the streets, to be applauded by people.
I assure you: They've got their reward! But when
you give to the poor, don't let your left hand know
what your right hand is doing, so that your giving
may be in secret. And your Father who sees in secret
will reward you.

Matthew 6:2-4 HCSB

A generous person will be enriched.

Proverbs 11:25 HCSB

Assuredly, I say to you, inasmuch as you did it to
one of the least of these My brethren, you did it to
Me.

Matthew 25:40 NKJV

So He called His disciples to Himself and said to them, "Assuredly, I say to you that this poor widow has put in more than all those who have given to the treasury; for they all put in out of their abundance, but she out of her poverty put in all that she had, her whole livelihood."

Mark 12:43-44 NKJV

Give, and it will be given to you; a good measure, pressed down, shaken together, and running over will be poured into your lap. For with the measure that you use, it will be measured back to you.

Luke 6:38 HCSB

The one who has two shirts must share with someone who has none, and the one who has food must do the same.

Luke 3:11 HCSB

Freely you have received, freely give.

Matthew 10:8 NKJV

If you want to be truly happy,
you won't find it on
an endless quest for more stuff.
You'll find it in receiving
God's generosity and in
passing that generosity along.

—

Bill Hybels

Chapter 5

Friends

I give thanks to my God
for every remembrance of you.

—

Philippians 1:3 HCSB

Friend: a one-syllable word describing "a person who is attached to another by feelings of affection or personal regard." This definition, or one very similar to it, can be found in any dictionary, but genuine friendship is much more. When we examine the deeper meaning of friendship, so many descriptors come to mind: trustworthiness, loyalty, helpfulness, kindness, understanding, forgiveness, encouragement, humor, and cheerfulness, to mention but a few.

Genuine friendship should be treasured and nurtured. As Christians, we are commanded to love one another. The familiar words of 1 Corinthians 13:2 remind us that love and charity are among God's greatest gifts: "And though I have the gift of prophecy, and understand all mysteries, and all knowledge; and though I have all faith, so that I could remove mountains, and have not charity, I am nothing" (KJV).

Today and every day, resolve to be a trustworthy, encouraging, loyal friend. And, treasure the people in your life who are loyal friends to you. Friendship is, after all, a glorious gift, praised by God. Give thanks for that gift and nurture it.

In friendship,
God opens your eyes
to the glories of Himself.

—

Joni Eareckson Tada

Don't bypass the potential for meaningful friendships just because of differences. Explore them. Embrace them. Love them.

Luci Swindoll

Yes, the Spirit was sent to be our Counselor. Yes, Jesus speaks to us personally. But often he works through another human being.

John Eldredge

Live in the present and make the most of your opportunities to enjoy your family and friends.

Barbara Johnson

God often keeps us on the path by guiding us through the counsel of friends and trusted spiritual advisors.

Bill Hybels

A friend is one who makes me do my best.

Oswald Chambers

We long to find someone who has been where we've been, who shares our fragile skies, who sees our sunsets with the same shades of blue.

Beth Moore

Friendship is one of the sweetest joys of life. Many might have failed beneath the bitterness of their trial had they not found a friend.

C. H. Spurgeon

Whenever we develop significant friendships with those who are not like us culturally, we become broader, wiser persons.

Richard Foster

The glory of friendship is not the outstretched hand, or the kindly smile, or the joy of companionship. It is the spiritual inspiration that comes to one when he discovers that someone else believes in him and is willing to trust him with his friendship.

Corrie ten Boom

Finally, all of you be of one mind,
having compassion
for one another; love as brothers,
be tenderhearted, be courteous.

—

1 Peter 3:8 NKJV

A friend loveth at all times, and a brother is born for adversity.

Proverbs 17:17 KJV

Oil and incense bring joy to the heart, and the sweetness of a friend is better than self-counsel.

Proverbs 27:9 HCSB

Beloved, if God so loved us, we also ought to love one another.

1 John 4:11 NKJV

Thine own friend, and thy father's friend, forsake not. . . .

Proverbs 27:10 KJV

The one who loves his brother remains in the light, and there is no cause for stumbling in him.

1 John 2:10 HCSB

Perhaps the greatest treasure
on earth and one of the only things
that will survive this life is human
relationships: old friends.
We are indeed rich if we have
friends. Friends who have loved us
through the problems and
heartaches of life.
Deep, true, joyful friendships.
Life is too short and eternity
too long to live without old friends.

—

Gloria Gaither

Chapter 6

Spending Time with Loved Ones

He has made everything appropriate in its time.
He has also put eternity in their hearts,
but man cannot discover the work
God has done from beginning to end.

—

Ecclesiastes 3:11 HCSB

It takes time to build strong relationships . . . lots of time. Yet we live in a world where time seems to be an ever-shrinking commodity as we rush from place to place with seldom a moment to spare.

Has the busy pace of life robbed you of sufficient time with your loved ones? If so, it's time to adjust your priorities. God can help.

When you fervently ask God to you help prioritize your life, He will give you guidance. When you seek His guidance every day, your Creator will reveal Himself in a variety of ways. As a follower of Christ, you must do no less.

When you allow God to help you organize your day, you'll soon discover that there is ample time for yourself and your family. When you make God a full partner in every aspect of your life, He will lead you along the proper path: His path. When you allow God to reign over your heart, He will honor you with spiritual blessings that are simply too numerous to count. So, as you plan for the day ahead, make God's priorities your priorities. When you do, every other priority will have a tendency to fall neatly into place.

Frustration is not the will of God. There is time to do anything and everything that God wants us to do.

Elisabeth Elliot

Our leisure, even our play, is a matter of serious concern. There is no neutral ground in the universe: every square inch, every split second, is claimed by God and counterclaimed by Satan.

C. S. Lewis

God has a present will for your life. It is neither chaotic nor utterly exhausting. In the midst of many good choices vying for your time, He will give you the discernment to recognize what is best.

Beth Moore

To choose time is to save time.

Francis Bacon

As we surrender the use of our time to the lordship of Christ, He will lead us to use it in the most productive way imaginable.

Charles Stanley

Our time is short! The time we can invest for God, in creative things, in receiving our fellowmen for Christ, is short!

Billy Graham

The work of God is appointed. There is always enough time to do the will of God.

Elisabeth Elliot

Finding time for God takes time . . . and it's up to you to find it.

Marie T. Freeman

The best use of life is love. The best expression of love is time. The best time to love is now.

Rick Warren

52

The more time you give
to something,
the more you reveal
its importance and
value to you.

—

Rick Warren

Therefore humble yourselves under the mighty hand of God, that He may exalt you in due time.

1 Peter 5:6 NKJV

He said to them, "It is not for you to know times or periods that the Father has set by His own authority."

Acts 1:7 HCSB

I wait for the Lord, my soul waits, and in His word I do hope. My soul waits for the Lord more than those who watch for the morning—Yes, more than those who watch for the morning.

Psalm 130:5-6 NKJV

I waited patiently for the Lord, and He turned to me and heard my cry for help. He brought me up from a desolate pit, out of the muddy clay, and set my feet on a rock, making my steps secure. He put a new song in my mouth, a hymn of praise to our God.

Psalm 40:1-3 HCSB

Therefore the Lord is waiting to show you mercy, and is rising up to show you compassion, for the Lord is a just God. Happy are all who wait patiently for Him.

Isaiah 30:18 HCSB

But those who wait on the LORD shall renew their strength; they shall mount up with wings like eagles, they shall run and not be weary, they shall walk and not faint.

Isaiah 40:31 NKJV

For My thoughts are not your thoughts, and your ways are not My ways. For as heaven is higher than earth, so My ways are higher than your ways, and My thoughts than your thoughts.

Isaiah 55:8-9 HCSB

The Lord is good to those who wait for Him, to the soul who seeks Him. It is good that one should hope and wait quietly for the salvation of the Lord.

Lamentations 3:25-26 NKJV

Overcommitment and time pressures are the greatest destroyers of marriages and families. It takes time to develop any friendship, whether with a loved one or with God himself.

—

James Dobson

Chapter 7

The Power of Encouragement

*I want their hearts to be encouraged
and joined together in love,
so that they may have all the riches
of assured understanding, and have
the knowledge of God's mystery—Christ.*

—

Colossians 2:2 HCSB

In the Book of Proverbs, we read that "A word spoken at the right time is like golden apples on a silver tray" (25:11 HCSB). This verse reminds us that the words we speak can and should be beautiful offerings to those we love.

All of us have the power to enrich the lives of our loved ones. Sometimes, when we feel uplifted and secure, we find it easy to speak words of encouragement and hope. Other times, when we are discouraged or tired, we can scarcely summon the energy to uplift ourselves, much less anyone else. But, as loving Christians, our obligation is clear: we must always measure our words carefully as we use them to benefit others and to glorify our Father in heaven.

God intends that we speak words of kindness, wisdom, and truth, no matter our circumstances, no matter our emotions. When we do, we share a priceless gift with our loved ones, and we give glory to the One who gave His life for us. As believers, we must do no less.

He climbs highest who helps another up.

Zig Ziglar

No journey is complete that does not lead through some dark valleys. We can properly comfort others only with the comfort we ourselves have been given by God.

Vance Havner

God is still in the process of dispensing gifts, and He uses ordinary individuals like us to develop those gifts in other people.

Howard Hendricks

The balance of affirmation and discipline, freedom and restraint, encouragement and warning is different for each child and season and generation, yet the absolutes of God's Word are necessary and trustworthy at all times.

Gloria Gaither

Encouragement starts at home, but it should never end there.

Marie T. Freeman

One of the ways God refills us after failure is through the blessing of Christian fellowship. Just experiencing the joy of simple activities shared with other children of God can have a healing effect on us.

Anne Graham Lotz

God grant that we may not hinder those who are battling their way slowly into the light.

Oswald Chambers

Make it a rule, and pray to God to help you to keep it, never to lie down at night without being able to say: "I have made at least one human being a little wiser, a little happier, or a little better this day."

Charles Kingsley

To the loved,
a word of affection
is a morsel,
but to the love-starved,
a word of affection
can be a feast.

—

Max Lucado

Carry one another's burdens; in this way you will fulfill the law of Christ.

Galatians 6:2 HCSB

But encourage each other daily, while it is still called today, so that none of you is hardened by sin's deception.

Hebrews 3:13 HCSB

And let us be concerned about one another in order to promote love and good works.

Hebrews 10:24 HCSB

Anxiety in a man's heart weighs it down, but a good word cheers it up.

Proverbs 12:25 HCSB

Iron sharpens iron, and one man sharpens another.

Proverbs 27:17 HCSB

*If anyone thinks he is religious,
without controlling his tongue
but deceiving his heart,
his religion is useless.*

—

James 1:26 HCSB

What are your
spouse's dreams?
What are you doing
to encourage or discourage
those dreams?

—

Dennis Swanberg

Chapter 8

Love and Laughter

There is an occasion for everything,
and a time for every activity under heaven . . .
a time to weep and a time to laugh;
a time to mourn and a time to dance.

—

Ecclesiastes 3:1, 4 HCSB

L aughter is a gift from God, a gift that He intends for us to use. Yet sometimes, because of the inevitable stresses of everyday living, we fail to find the fun in life. When we allow life's inevitable disappointments to cast a pall over our lives and our souls, we do a profound disservice to ourselves and to our loved ones.

If you've allowed the clouds of life to obscure the blessings of life, perhaps you've formed the unfortunate habit of taking things just a little too seriously. If so, it's time to fret a little less and laugh a little more.

So today, look for the humor that most certainly surrounds you and your loved ones. Remember: God created laughter for a reason . . . and Father indeed knows best. So laugh!

We may run, walk, stumble, drive, or fly, but let us never lose sight of the reason for the journey, or miss a chance to see a rainbow on the way.

Gloria Gaither

The people whom I have seen succeed best in life have always been cheerful and hopeful people who went about their business with a smile on their faces.

Charles Kingsley

Christ can put a spring in your step and a thrill in your heart. Optimism and cheerfulness are products of knowing Christ.

Billy Graham

If you want people to feel comfortable around you, to enjoy being with you, then learn to laugh at yourself and find humor in life's little mishaps.

Dennis Swanberg

He who laughs lasts—he who doesn't, doesn't.

Marie T. Freeman

I think everybody ought to be a laughing Christian. I'm convinced that there's just one place where there's not any laughter, and that's hell.

Jerry Clower

Laughter is to life what shock absorbers are to automobiles. It won't take the potholes out of the road, but it sure makes the ride smoother.

Barbara Johnson

It is pleasing to the dear God whenever you rejoice or laugh from the bottom of your heart.

Martin Luther

God is good, and heaven is forever. And if those two facts don't cheer you up, nothing will.

Marie T. Freeman

When we bring sunshine
into the lives of others,
we're warmed by it ourselves.
When we spill
a little happiness,
it splashes on us.

—

Barbara Johnson

I will thank the Lord
with all my heart; I will declare
all Your wonderful works.
I will rejoice and boast about You;
I will sing about Your name,
Most High.

—

Psalm 9:1-2 HCSB

Happy are the people whose strength is in You, whose hearts are set on pilgrimage.

Psalm 84:5 HCSB

Happy is the one whose help is the God of Jacob, whose hope is in the Lord his God.

Psalm 146:5 HCSB

My lips will shout for joy when I sing praise to You.

Psalm 71:23 HCSB

A joyful heart makes a face cheerful.

Proverbs 15:13 HCSB

Oh, clap your hands, all you peoples! Shout to God with the voice of triumph!

Psalm 47:1 NKJV

The Lord reigns; let the earth rejoice.

Psalm 97:1 NKJV

A little comic relief in
a discussion does no harm,
however serious the topic
may be. (In my own
experience the funniest things
have occurred in
the gravest and most sincere
conversations.)

—

C. S. Lewis

Chapter 9

Love Requires Patience

A patient spirit is better than a proud spirit.

—

Ecclesiastes 7:8 HCSB

L oving relationships inevitably require patience . . . plenty of patience.

We live in an imperfect world inhabited by imperfect people, and we need to be patient with everybody, especially our loved ones. Most of us, however, are perfectly willing to be patient with our spouses just as long as things unfold according to our own plans and according to our own timetables. In other words, we know precisely what we want, and we know precisely when we want it: right now, if not sooner.

As the old saying goes, "God gave everyone patience—wise people use it." But, for most of us, being patient with other folks is difficult. Why? Because we (like the "other folks") are fallible human beings, sometimes quick to anger and sometimes slow to forgive.

The next time you find your patience tested to the limit, slow down, calm down, and pray for guidance. And remember this: sometimes, we must wait patiently for our loved ones, and sometimes we must wait patiently for God. And that's as it should be. After all, think how patient God has been with us.

Waiting is an essential part of spiritual discipline. It can be the ultimate test of faith.

Anne Graham Lotz

God never hurries. There are no deadlines against which He must work. To know this is to quiet our spirits and relax our nerves.

A. W. Tozer

The deepest spiritual lessons are not learned by His letting us have our way in the end, but by His making us wait, bearing with us in love and patience until we are able honestly to pray what He taught His disciples to pray: Thy will be done.

Elisabeth Elliot

Waiting means going about our assigned tasks, confident that God will provide the meaning and the conclusions.

Eugene Peterson

No matter what we are going through, no matter how long the waiting for answers, of one thing we may be sure. God is faithful. He keeps His promises. What He starts, He finishes . . . including His perfect work in us.

Gloria Gaither

It is wise to wait because God gives clear direction only when we are willing to wait.

Charles Stanley

Let me encourage you to continue to wait with faith. God may not perform a miracle, but He is trustworthy to touch you and make you whole where there used to be a hole.

Lisa Whelchel

When there is perplexity there is always guidance—not always at the moment we ask, but in good time, which is God's time. There is no need to fret and stew.

Elisabeth Elliot

Those who have had to wait
and work for happiness
seem to enjoy it more,
because they never
take it for granted.

—

Barbara Johnson

Now we exhort you, brethren, warn those who are unruly, comfort the fainthearted, uphold the weak, be patient with all.

1 Thessalonians 5:14 NKJV

For ye have need of patience, that, after ye have done the will of God, ye might receive the promise.

Hebrews 10:36 KJV

Therefore the Lord is waiting to show you mercy, and is rising up to show you compassion, for the Lord is a just God. Happy are all who wait patiently for Him.

Isaiah 30:18 HCSB

My dearly loved brothers, understand this: everyone must be quick to hear, slow to speak, and slow to anger, for man's anger does not accomplish God's righteousness.

James 1:19-20 HCSB

*A patient person [shows] great understanding, but a
quick-tempered one promotes foolishness.*

Proverbs 14:29 HCSB

Wait on the Lord, and He will rescue you.

Proverbs 20:22 HCSB

*I wait for the Lord; I wait, and put my hope in His
word.*

Psalm 130:5 HCSB

*A person's insight gives him patience, and his virtue
is to overlook an offense.*

Proverbs 19:11 HCSB

If you want to hear
God's voice clearly and you are
uncertain, then remain in
His presence until He changes
that uncertainty.
Often much can happen
during this waiting for the Lord.
Sometimes he changes pride
into humility; doubt into
faith and peace.

—

Corrie ten Boom

Chapter 10

Love Requires Truth

You will know the truth,
and the truth will set you free.

—

John 8:32 HCSB

Great relationships are built on a foundation of trust. Without trust, relationships of every kind tend to wither on the vine; with trust, relationships don't just grow; they flourish.

It's been said on many occasions that honesty is the best policy. For believers, it's far more important to note that honesty is God's policy. And, if we are to be servants worthy of our Savior, Jesus Christ, we must be honest and forthright in all our communications with all people, starting with our loved ones. God's Word is clear: "Lying lips are an abomination to the Lord, but those who deal truthfully are His delight" (Proverbs 12:22 NKJV).

In the Book of Exodus, God did not command, "Thou shalt not bear false witness when it is convenient." And He didn't say, "Thou shalt not bear false witness most of the time." God said, "Thou shalt not bear false witness" period—no "ifs, ands, or buts."

Sometime soon, perhaps even today, you will be tempted to start monkeyin' with the truth . . . you know what I mean: to bend it, stretch it, shape it, or break it. Resist that temptation. Truth is God's way . . . and it must be your way, too.

Do you want relationships that can stand the test of time? Then build your relationships upon mutual trust and unerring truth. It's the only decent way to love.

Truth is always about something, but reality is that about which truth is.

—

C. S. Lewis

We have in Jesus Christ a perfect example of how to put God's truth into practice.

Bill Bright

For Christians, God himself is the only absolute; truth and ethics are rooted in his character.

Charles Colson

Truth will triumph. The Father of truth will win, and the followers of truth will be saved.

Max Lucado

Only Jesus Christ is the truth for everyone who has ever been born into the human race, regardless of culture, age, nationality, generation, heritage, gender, color, or language.

Anne Graham Lotz

Those who walk in truth walk in liberty.

Beth Moore

God will see to it that we understand as much truth as we are willing to obey.

Elisabeth Elliot

Learning God's truth and getting it into our heads is one thing, but living God's truth and getting it into our characters is quite something else.

Warren Wiersbe

The temple of truth has never suffered so much from the wood-peckers on the outside as from termites within.

Vance Havner

If the price of which you shall have a true experience is that of sorrow, buy the truth at that price.

C. H. Spurgeon

"You are a king then?" Pilate asked.
"You say that I'm a king,"
Jesus replied. "I was born for this,
and I have come into the world for
this: to testify to the truth.
Everyone who is of the truth
listens to My voice."

—

John 18:37 HCSB

86

You have already heard about this hope in the message of truth, the gospel that has come to you. It is bearing fruit and growing all over the world, just as it has among you since the day you heard it and recognized God's grace in the truth.

Colossians 1:5-6 HCSB

When the Spirit of truth comes, He will guide you into all the truth.

John 16:13 HCSB

These are the things you must do: Speak truth to one another; render honest and peaceful judgments in your gates.

Zechariah 8:16 HCSB

I have no greater joy than this: to hear that my children are walking in the truth.

3 John 1:4 HCSB

The best evidence of
our having the truth is our
walking in the truth.

—

Matthew Henry

Chapter 11

Praying for Our Loved Ones

The intense prayer of the righteous is very powerful.

—

James 5:16 HCSB

Jesus made it clear to His disciples: they should pray always. And so should we. Genuine, heartfelt prayer changes things and it changes us. When we lift our hearts to our Father in heaven, we open ourselves to a never-ending source of divine wisdom, limitless power, and infinite love.

Today, we offer a prayer of thanks to God for our loved ones. Loyal Christian friends and family members have much to offer us: encouragement, faith, fellowship, and fun, for starters. And when we align ourselves with godly believers, we are blessed by them and by our Creator.

Let us thank God for all the people who love us—for the people He has placed along our paths. And let's pray for our family and friends with sincere hearts. God hears our prayers, and He responds.

A life growing in its purity and devotion will be a more prayerful life.

E. M. Bounds

God knows that we, with our limited vision, don't even know that for which we should pray. When we entrust our requests to him, we trust him to honor our prayers with holy judgment.

Max Lucado

Prayer guards hearts and minds and causes God to bring peace out of chaos.

Beth Moore

What of the great prayer Jesus taught us to pray? It is for His kingdom and His will, yet we ought not to ask it unless we ourselves are prepared to cooperate.

Elisabeth Elliot

Two wings are necessary to lift our souls toward God: prayer and praise. Prayer asks. Praise accepts the answer.

Mrs. Charles E. Cowman

Find a place to pray where no one imagines that you are praying. Then, shut the door and talk to God.

Oswald Chambers

Prayer connects us with God's limitless potential.

Henry Blackaby

Wasted time of which we are later ashamed, temptations we yield to, weaknesses, lethargy in our work, disorder and lack of discipline in our thoughts and in our interaction with others—all these frequently have their root in neglecting prayer in the morning.

Dietrich Bonhoeffer

To pray is to mount on eagle's wings above the clouds and get into the clear heaven where God dwells.

C. H. Spurgeon

We forget that God sometimes has to say "No." We pray to Him as our heavenly Father, and like wise human fathers, He often says, "No," not from whim or caprice, but from wisdom, from love, and from knowing what is best for us.

Peter Marshall

I learned as never before that persistent calling upon the Lord breaks through every stronghold of the devil, for nothing is impossible with God. For Christians in these troubled times, there is simply no other way.

Jim Cymbala

Let the words of my mouth and the meditation of my heart be acceptable in Your sight, O Lord, my strength and my Redeemer.

Psalm 19:14 NKJV

Yet He often withdrew to deserted places and prayed.

Luke 5:16 HCSB

Don't worry about anything, but in everything, through prayer and petition with thanksgiving, let your requests be made known to God.

Philippians 4:6 HCSB

Rejoice in hope; be patient in affliction; be persistent in prayer.

Romans 12:12 HCSB

And everything—whatever you ask in prayer, believing—you will receive.

Matthew 21:22 HCSB

94

Rejoice always! Pray constantly. Give thanks in everything, for this is God's will for you in Christ Jesus.

1 Thessalonians 5:16-18 HCSB

I sought the LORD, and he heard me, and delivered me from all my fears.

Psalm 34:4 KJV

Therefore I want the men in every place to pray, lifting up holy hands without anger or argument.

1 Timothy 2:8 HCSB

Only God can move
mountains,
but faith and prayer
can move God.

—

E. M. Bounds

Chapter 12

Love Requires Forgiveness

Then Jesus said, "Father, forgive them,
for they do not know what they do."
And they divided His garments and cast lots.

—

Luke 23:34 NKJV

How often must we forgive family members and friends? More times than we can count. Our children are precious but imperfect; so are our spouses and our friends. We must, on occasion, forgive those who have injured us; to do otherwise is to disobey God.

Are you easily frustrated by the inevitable imperfections of others? Are you a prisoner of bitterness and regret? If so, perhaps you need a refresher course in the art of forgiveness.

If there exists even one person, alive or dead, whom you have not forgiven (and that includes yourself), follow God's commandment and His will for your life: forgive. Bitterness, anger, and regret are not part of God's plan for your life. Forgiveness is.

As you have received the mercy of God by the forgiveness of sin and the promise of eternal life, thus you must show mercy.

Billy Graham

Our relationships with other people are of primary importance to God. Because God is love, He cannot tolerate any unforgiveness or hardness in us toward any individual.

Catherine Marshall

Forgiveness is not an emotion. Forgiveness is an act of the will, and the will can function regardless of the temperature of the heart.

Corrie ten Boom

I firmly believe a great many prayers are not answered because we are not willing to forgive someone.

D. L. Moody

Revenge is the raging fire that consumes the arsonist.

Max Lucado

Only the truly forgiven are truly forgiving.

C. S. Lewis

Forgiveness is actually the best revenge because it not only sets us free from the person we forgive, but it frees us to move into all that God has in store for us.

Stormie Omartian

We are products of our past, but we don't have to be prisoners of it. God specializes in giving people a fresh start.

Rick Warren

To hold on to hate and resentments is to throw a monkey wrench into the machinery of life.

E. Stanley Jones

It is better to
forgive and forget
than to
resent and remember.

—

Barbara Johnson

When they persisted in questioning Him, He stood up and said to them, "The one without sin among you should be the first to throw a stone at her."

John 8:7 HCSB

Do not judge, and you will not be judged. Do not condemn, and you will not be condemned. Forgive, and you will be forgiven.

Luke 6:37 HCSB

Then Peter came to Him and said, "Lord, how many times could my brother sin against me and I forgive him? As many as seven times?" "I tell you, not as many as seven," Jesus said to him, "but 70 times seven."

Matthew 18:21-22 HCSB

And be kind to one another, tenderhearted, forgiving one another, just as God in Christ forgave you.

Ephesians 4:32 NKJV

A person's insight gives him patience, and his virtue is to overlook an offense.

Proverbs 19:11 HCSB

You have heard that it was said, You shall love your neighbor and hate your enemy. But I tell you, love your enemies, and pray for those who persecute you, so that you may be sons of your Father in heaven.

Matthew 5:43-45 HCSB

And forgive us our sins, for we ourselves also forgive everyone in debt to us.

Luke 11:4 HCSB

And whenever you stand praying, if you have anything against anyone, forgive him, so that your Father in heaven may also forgive you your wrongdoing.

Mark 11:25 HCSB

God expects us to forgive
others as He has forgiven us;
we are to follow His example
by having a forgiving heart.

—

Vonette Bright

Chapter 13

Growing Together

But grow in the grace and knowledge
of our Lord and Savior Jesus Christ.
To Him be the glory both now
and to the day of eternity.

—

2 Peter 3:18 HCSB

As Christians, we can—and should—never stop growing in the love and knowledge of our Savior.

When we cease to grow, either emotionally or spiritually, we do ourselves and our loved ones a profound disservice. But, if we study God's Word, if we obey His commandments, and if we live in the center of His will, we will not be "stagnant" believers; we will, instead, be growing Christians . . . and that's exactly what God wants for our lives and our relationships.

Many of life's most important lessons are painful to learn. Thankfully, during times of heartbreak and hardship, God stands ready to protect us. As Psalm 46:1 promises, "God is our protection and our strength. He always helps in times of trouble" (NCV). In His own time and according to His master plan, God will heal us if we invite Him into our hearts.

Spiritual growth need not take place only in times of adversity. We must seek to grow in our knowledge and love of the Lord every day that we live. In those quiet moments when we open our hearts to God, the One who made us keeps remaking us. He gives us direction, perspective, wisdom, and courage. And, the appropriate moment to accept those spiritual gifts is always the present one.

I'm not what I want to be.
I'm not what I'm going to be.
But, thank God,
I'm not what I was!

—

Gloria Gaither

Some people have received Christ but have never reached spiritual maturity. We should grow as Christians every day, and we are not completely mature until we live in the presence of Christ.

Billy Graham

We had plenty of challenges, some of which were tremendously serious, yet God has enabled us to walk, crawl, limp, or leap—whatever way we could progress—toward wholeness.

Beth Moore

Growth in depth and strength and consistency and fruitfulness and ultimately in Christlikeness is only possible when the winds of life are contrary to personal comfort.

Anne Graham Lotz

I do not know how the Spirit of Christ performs it, but He brings us choices through which we constantly change, fresh and new, into His likeness.

Joni Eareckson Tada

Recently I've been learning that life comes down to this: God is in everything. Regardless of what difficulties I am experiencing at the moment, or what things aren't as I would like them to be, I look at the circumstances and say, "Lord, what are you trying to teach me?"

Catherine Marshall

I've never met anyone who became instantly mature. It's a painstaking process that God takes us through, and it includes such things as waiting, failing, losing, and being misunderstood—each calling for extra doses of perseverance.

Charles Swindoll

God wants to revolutionize our lives—by showing us how knowing Him can be the most powerful force to help us become all we want to be.

Bill Hybels

For this reason also, since the day we heard this, we haven't stopped praying for you. We are asking that you may be filled with the knowledge of His will in all wisdom and spiritual understanding.

Colossians 1:9 HCSB

Therefore, leaving the elementary message about the Messiah, let us go on to maturity.

Hebrews 6:1 HCSB

I want their hearts to be encouraged and joined together in love, so that they may have all the riches of assured understanding, and have the knowledge of God's mystery—Christ.

Colossians 2:2 HCSB

For You, O God, have tested us; You have refined us as silver is refined. You brought us into the net; You laid affliction on our backs. You have caused men to ride over our heads; we went through fire and through water; but You brought us out to rich fulfillment.

Psalm 66:10–12 NKJV

*Like newborn infants,
desire the unadulterated
spiritual milk, so that you may
grow by it in your salvation.*

—

1 Peter 2:2 HCSB

Walking in faith brings you
to the Word of God.
There you will be healed,
cleansed, fed, nurtured,
equipped, and matured.

—

Kay Arthur

Chapter 14

The Right Words

Pleasant words are a honeycomb:
sweet to the taste and health to the body.

—

Proverbs 16:24 HCSB

All too often, we underestimate the importance of the words we speak. Whether we realize it or not, our words carry great weight and great power, especially when we are addressing our loved ones.

Christ taught that "Out of the abundance of the heart the mouth speaks" (Matthew 12:34 NKJV). Does the abundance of your heart produce a continuing flow of encouraging words for your loved ones? And, are you willing to hold your tongue when you feel the urge to begin an angry outburst? Hopefully so. After all, sometimes the most important words are the ones you don't speak.

If you want to build better relationships—and if you want to keep building them day by day—think first and talk next. Avoid angry outbursts. Refrain from constant criticism. Terminate tantrums. Negate negativism. Cease cynicism. Instead, use Christ as your guide, and speak words of encouragement, hope, praise, and, above all, love—and speak them often.

We should ask ourselves three things before we speak: Is it true? Is it kind? Does it glorify God?

Billy Graham

Fill the heart with the love of Christ so that only truth and purity can come out of the mouth.

Warren Wiersbe

Part of good communication is listening with the eyes as well as with the ears.

Josh McDowell

Attitude and the spirit in which we communicate are as important as the words we say.

Charles Stanley

The fewer words, the better prayer.

Martin Luther

Does your message end with one point like a sword, or does it end like a broom with a thousand straws?

Vance Havner

Like dynamite, God's power is only latent power until it is released. You can release God's dynamite power into people's lives and the world through faith, your words, and prayer.

Bill Bright

When you talk, choose the very same words that you would use if Jesus were looking over your shoulder. Because He is.

Marie T. Freeman

The things that we feel most deeply we ought to learn to be silent about, at least until we have talked them over thoroughly with God.

Elisabeth Elliot

Change the heart,
and you change the speech.

—

Warren Wiersbe

There is one who speaks rashly, like a piercing sword; but the tongue of the wise [brings] healing.

Proverbs 12:18 HCSB

For the one who wants to love life and to see good days must keep his tongue from evil and his lips from speaking deceit.

1 Peter 3:10 HCSB

Avoid irreverent, empty speech, for this will produce an even greater measure of godlessness.

2 Timothy 2:16 HCSB

No rotten talk should come from your mouth, but only what is good for the building up of someone in need, in order to give grace to those who hear.

Ephesians 4:29 HCSB

Lord, set up a guard for my mouth; keep watch at the door of my lips.

Psalm 141:3 HCSB

If anyone thinks he is religious, without controlling his tongue but deceiving his heart, his religion is useless.

James 1:26 HCSB

I tell you that on the day of judgment people will have to account for every careless word they speak. For by your words you will be acquitted, and by your words you will be condemned.

Matthew 12:36-37 HCSB

Therefore, laying aside all malice, all deceit, hypocrisy, envy, and all evil speaking, as newborn babes, desire the pure milk of the word, that you may grow thereby.

1 Peter 2:1-2 NKJV

A little kindly advice is better
than a great deal of scolding.

—

Fanny Crosby

Chapter 15

Your Family

*Choose for yourselves today the one
you will worship. . . . As for me and my family,
we will worship the Lord.*

—

Joshua 24:15 HCSB

A loving family is a treasure from God. If God has blessed you with a close-knit, supportive clan, offer a word of thanks to your Creator because He has given you one of His most precious earthly possessions. Your obligation, in response to God's gift, is to treat your family in ways that are consistent with His commandments.

When you place God squarely in the center of your family's life—when you worship Him, praise Him, trust Him, and love Him—then He will most certainly bless you and yours in ways that you could have scarcely imagined.

So the next time your family life becomes a little stressful, remember this: That little band of men, women, kids, and babies is a priceless treasure on temporary loan from the Father above. And it's your responsibility to praise God for that gift—and to act accordingly.

The only true source of meaning in life is found in love for God and his son Jesus Christ, and love for mankind, beginning with our own families.

James Dobson

There is so much compassion and understanding that is gained when we've experienced God's grace firsthand within our own families.

Lisa Whelchel

Calm and peaceful, the home should be the one place where people are certain they will be welcomed, received, protected, and loved.

Ed Young

A family is a place where principles are hammered and honed on the anvil of everyday living.

Charles Swindoll

Apart from religious influence, the family is the most important influence on society.

Billy Graham

I like to think of my family as a big, beautiful patchwork quilt—each of us so different yet stitched together by love and life experiences.

Barbara Johnson

Sadly, family problems and even financial problems are seldom the real problem, but often the symptom of a weak or nonexistent value system.

Dave Ramsey

A home is a place where we find direction.

Gigi Graham Tchividjian

Examine yourselves—ask, each of you, "Have I been a good brother? . . . son? . . . husband? . . . father? . . . servant?"

Charles Kingsley

Never give your family
the leftovers and crumbs
of your time.

—

Charles Swindoll

If a kingdom is divided against itself, that kingdom cannot stand. If a house is divided against itself, that house cannot stand.

Mark 3:24-25 HCSB

The one who brings ruin on his household will inherit the wind.

Proverbs 11:29 HCSB

Unless the Lord builds a house, its builders labor over it in vain; unless the Lord watches over a city, the watchman stays alert in vain.

Psalm 127:1 HCSB

Love must be without hypocrisy. Detest evil; cling to what is good. Show family affection to one another with brotherly love. Outdo one another in showing honor.

Romans 12:9-10 HCSB

If I speak the languages of men and of angels, but do not have love, I am a sounding gong or a clanging cymbal.

1 Corinthians 13:1 HCSB

Dear friends, if God loved us in this way, we also must love one another.

1 John 4:11 HCSB

Love one another earnestly from a pure heart.

1 Peter 1:22 HCSB

Do not be unequally yoked together with unbelievers. For what fellowship has righteousness with lawlessness? And what communion has light with darkness?

2 Corinthians 6:14 NKJV

The miraculous thing about
being a family is that
in the last analysis, we are
each dependent of one another
and God, woven together
by mercy given
and mercy received.

—

Barbara Johnson

Chapter 16

The Right Kind of Attitude

Finally brothers, whatever is true,
whatever is honorable,
whatever is just, whatever is pure,
whatever is lovely, whatever is commendable—
if there is any moral excellence
and if there is any praise—dwell on these things.

—

Philippians 4:8 HCSB

How will you direct your thoughts today? Will you obey the words of Philippians 4:8 by dwelling upon those things that are honorable, true, and worthy of praise? Or will you allow your thoughts to be hijacked by the negativity that seems to dominate our troubled world? Are you fearful, angry, bored, or worried? Are you so preoccupied with the concerns of this day that you fail to thank God for the promise of eternity? Are you confused, bitter, or pessimistic? If so, God wants to have a little talk with you.

God intends that you experience joy and abundance, but He will not force His joy upon you; you must claim it for yourself. So, today and every day hereafter, celebrate this life that God has given you by focusing your thoughts and your energies upon "whatever is of good repute." Today, count your blessings instead of your hardships. And thank the Giver of all things good for gifts that are simply too numerous to count.

Attitude is an inward feeling expressed by behavior.

John Maxwell

It's your choice: you can either count your blessings or recount your disappointments.

Jim Gallery

The purity of motive determines the quality of action.

Oswald Chambers

If the attitude of servanthood is learned, by attending to God as Lord. Then, serving others will develop as a very natural way of life.

Eugene Peterson

Life is 10% what happens to you and 90% how you respond to it.

Charles Swindoll

I could go through this day oblivious to the miracles all around me, or I could tune in and "enjoy."

Gloria Gaither

You've heard the saying, "Life is what you make it." That means we have a choice. We can choose to have a life full of frustration and fear, but we can just as easily choose one of joy and contentment.

Dennis Swanberg

Attitude is the mind's paintbrush; it can color any situation.

Barbara Johnson

The Reference Point for the Christian is the Bible. All values, judgments, and attitudes must be gauged in relationship to this Reference Point.

Ruth Bell Graham

No matter how little we can change about our circumstances, we always have a choice about our attitude toward the situation.

Vonette Bright

"If the Lord will" is not just a statement on a believer's lips; it is the constant attitude of his heart.

Warren Wiersbe

The things we think are the things that feed our souls. If we think on pure and lovely things, we shall grow pure and lovely like them; and the converse is equally true.

Hannah Whitall Smith

Set your minds on what is above, not on what is on the earth.

Colossians 3:2 HCSB

For the word of God is living and powerful, and sharper than any two-edged sword, piercing even to the division of soul and spirit, and of joints and marrow, and is a discerner of the thoughts and intents of the heart.

Hebrews 4:12 NKJV

Make your own attitude that of Christ Jesus.

Philippians 2:5 HCSB

Don't work only while being watched, in order to please men, but as slaves of Christ, do God's will from your heart. Render service with a good attitude, as to the Lord and not to men.

Ephesians 6:6-7 HCSB

May the words of my mouth and the meditation of my heart be acceptable to You, Lord, my rock and my Redeemer.

Psalm 19:14 HCSB

Guard your heart above all else, for it is the source of life.

Proverbs 4:23 HCSB

I, the Lord, examine the mind, I test the heart to give to each according to his way, according to what his actions deserve.

Jeremiah 17:10 HCSB

As for you, Solomon my son, know the God of your father, and serve Him with a whole heart and a willing mind, for the Lord searches every heart and understands the intention of every thought. If you seek Him, He will be found by you, but if you forsake Him, He will reject you forever.

1 Chronicles 28:9 HCSB

I have witnessed
many attitudes
make a positive turnaround
through prayer.

—

John Maxwell

Chapter 17

Sharing the Joy

But let all who take refuge in You rejoice.

—

Psalm 5:11 HCSB

Oswald Chambers correctly observed, "Joy is the great note all throughout the Bible." C. S. Lewis echoed that thought when he wrote, "Joy is the serious business of heaven." But, even the most dedicated Christians can, on occasion, forget to celebrate each day for what it is: a priceless gift from God.

Today, let us be joyful Christians with smiles on our faces and kind words on our lips. After all, this is God's day, and He has given us clear instructions for its use. We are commanded to rejoice and be glad. So, with no further ado, let the celebration begin . . .

If you can forgive the person you were, accept the person you are, and believe in the person you will become, you are headed for joy. So celebrate your life.

Barbara Johnson

The Christian lifestyle is not one of legalistic do's and don'ts, but one that is positive, attractive, and joyful.

Vonette Bright

Joy is the direct result of having God's perspective on our daily lives and the effect of loving our Lord enough to obey His commands and trust His promises.

Bill Bright

Our sense of joy, satisfaction, and fulfillment in life increases, no matter what the circumstances, if we are in the center of God's will.

Billy Graham

Joy is the heart's harmonious response to the Lord's song of love.

A. W. Tozer

Lord, I thank you for the promise of heaven and the unexpected moments when you touch my heartstrings with that longing for my eternal home.

Joni Eareckson Tada

Joy in life is not the absence of sorrow. The fact that Jesus could have joy in the midst of sorrow is proof that we can experience this too.

Warren Wiersbe

God knows everything. He can manage everything, and He loves us. Surely this is enough for a fullness of joy that is beyond words.

Hannah Whitall Smith

God gives to us a heavenly gift called joy, radically different in quality from any natural joy.

Elisabeth Elliot

Rejoice, the Lord is King; Your Lord and King adore! Rejoice, give thanks and sing and triumph evermore.

Charles Wesley

The Christian should be an alleluia from head to foot!

St. Augustine

Some of us seem so anxious about avoiding hell that we forget to celebrate our journey toward heaven.

Philip Yancey

Delight yourself also in the Lord, and He shall give you the desires of your heart.

Psalm 37:4 NKJV

Rejoice evermore. Pray without ceasing. In every thing give thanks: for this is the will of God in Christ Jesus concerning you.

1 Thessalonians 5:16-18 KJV

Rejoice in the Lord, you righteous ones; praise from the upright is beautiful.

Psalm 33:1 HCSB

Weeping may endure for a night, but joy comes in the morning.

Psalm 30:5 NKJV

But now I come to You, and these things I speak in the world, that they may have My joy fulfilled in themselves.

John 17:13 NKJV

Rejoice in the Lord always.
I will say it again: Rejoice!
—

Philippians 4:4 HCSB

A life of intimacy with God is characterized by joy.

—

Oswald Chambers

Chapter 18

Becoming a Humble Servant

There are different kinds of gifts, but they are all from the same Spirit. There are different ways to serve but the same Lord to serve.

—

1 Corinthians 12:4–5 NCV

We live in a world that glorifies power, prestige, fame, and money. But the words of Jesus teach us that the most esteemed men and women are not the widely acclaimed leaders of society; the most esteemed among us are the humble servants of society.

When we experience success, it's easy to puff out our chests and proclaim, "I did that!" But it's wrong. Whatever "it" is, God did it, and He deserves the credit. As Christians, we have been refashioned and saved by Jesus Christ, and that salvation came not because of our own good works but because of God's grace.

Dietrich Bonhoeffer was correct when he observed, "It is very easy to overestimate the importance of our own achievements in comparison with what we owe others." In other words, reality breeds humility.

Are you willing to become a humble servant for Christ? Are you willing to pitch in and make the world a better place, or are you determined to keep all your blessings to yourself? The answer to these questions will determine the quantity and the quality of the service you render to God—and to His children.

Today, you may feel the temptation to take more than you give. You may be tempted to withhold your generosity. Or you may be tempted to build yourself up in the eyes of your friends. Resist these temptations. Instead, serve your friends quietly and without fanfare. Find a need and fill it . . . humbly. Lend a helping hand . . . anonymously. Share a word of kindness . . . with quiet sincerity. As you go about your daily activities, remember that the Savior of all humanity made Himself a servant, and you, as His follower, must do no less.

In God's family, there is to be one great body of people: servants. In fact, that's the way to the top in His kingdom.

—

Charles Swindoll

Before the judgment seat of Christ, my service will not be judged by how much I have done but by how much of me there is in it.

A. W. Tozer

My heart's desire is to find more opportunities to give myself away and teach my children the joy of service at the same time.

Liz Curtis Higgs

So many times we say that we can't serve God because we aren't whatever is needed. We're not talented enough or smart enough or whatever. But if you are in covenant with Jesus Christ, He is responsible for covering your weaknesses, for being your strength. He will give you His abilities for your disabilities!

Kay Arthur

In Jesus, the service of God and the service of the least of the brethren were one.

Dietrich Bonhoeffer

God has lots of folks who intend to go to work for him "some day." What He needs is more people who are willing to work for Him today.

Marie T. Freeman

In the very place where God has put us, whatever its limitations, whatever kind of work it may be, we may indeed serve the Lord Christ.

Elisabeth Elliot

If you want to discover your spiritual gifts, start obeying God. As you serve Him, you will find that He has given you the gifts that are necessary to follow through in obedience.

Anne Graham Lotz

When you're enjoying the fulfillment and fellowship that inevitably accompanies authentic service, ministry is a joy. Instead of exhausting you, it energizes you; instead of burnout, you experience blessing.

Bill Hybels

149

So prepare your minds for service and have self-control. All your hope should be for the gift of grace that will be yours when Jesus Christ is shown to you.

1 Peter 1:13 NCV

Therefore, since we receive a kingdom which cannot be shaken, let us show gratitude, by which we may offer to God an acceptable service with reverence and awe.

Hebrews 12:28 NASB

If they serve Him obediently, they will end their days in prosperity and their years in happiness.

Job 36:11 HCSB

A person should consider us in this way: as servants of Christ and managers of God's mysteries. In this regard, it is expected of managers that each one be found faithful.

1 Corinthians 4:1-2 HCSB

Worship the Lord your God and . . . serve Him only.

Matthew 4:10 HCSB

Whoever serves me must follow me. Then my servant will be with me everywhere I am. My Father will honor anyone who serves me.

John 12:26 NCV

A kind man benefits himself, but a cruel man brings disaster on himself.

Proverbs 11:17 HCSB

Verily I say unto you, inasmuch as ye have done it unto one of the least of these my brethren, ye have done it unto me.

Matthew 25:40 KJV

Make it a rule, and pray to
God to help you to keep it,
never, if possible,
to lie down at night without
being able to say:
"I have made one human being
at least a little wiser,
or a little happier, or at least
a little better this day."

—

Charles Kingsley

Chapter 19

The Wisdom to Be Humble

Clothe yourselves with humility toward one another, because God resists the proud, but gives grace to the humble.

—

1 Peter 5:5 HCSB

We have heard the phrases on countless occasions: "He's a self-made man," or "she's a self-made woman." In truth, none of us are self-made. We all owe countless debts that we can never repay.

Our first debt, of course, is to our Father in heaven—Who has given us everything—and to His Son Who sacrificed His own life so that we might live eternally. We are also indebted to ancestors, parents, teachers, friends, spouses, family members, coworkers, fellow believers . . . and the list, of course, goes on.

As Christians, we have a profound reason to be humble: We have been refashioned and saved by Jesus Christ, and that salvation came not because of our own good works but because of God's grace. Thus, we are not "self-made"; we are "God-made" and "Christ-saved." How, then, can we be boastful? The answer, of course, is that, if we are honest with ourselves and with our God, we simply can't be boastful . . . we must, instead, be eternally grateful and exceedingly humble.

Humility is not, in most cases, a naturally occurring human trait. Most of us, it seems, are more than willing to stick out our chests and say, "Look at me; I did that!" But in our better moments, in the quiet moments when we search the depths of our own hearts, we know better. Whatever "it" is, God did that, not us.

St. Augustine observed, "If you plan to build a tall house of virtues, you must first lay deep foundations of humility." Are you a believer who genuinely seeks to build your house of virtues on a strong foundation of humility? If so, you are wise and you are blessed. But if you've been laboring under the misconception that you're a "self-made" man or woman, it's time to face facts: your blessings come from God. And He deserves the credit.

If you know who you are in Christ,
your personal ego is not an issue.

—

Beth Moore

I can usually sense that a leading is from the Holy Spirit when it calls me to humble myself, to serve somebody, to encourage somebody, or to give something away. Very rarely will the evil one lead us to do those kind of things.

Bill Hybels

The gate of heaven is very low; only the humble can enter it.

Elizabeth Ann Seton

As children observe an attitude and spirit of humility in us, our example will pave the way for them when they must admit to their heavenly Father their own desperate need for guidance and forgiveness.

Annie Chapman

As a ship cannot be built without nails, so a person cannot be saved without humility.

Amma Syncletice

Because Christ Jesus came to the world clothed in humility, he will always be found among those who are clothed with humility. He will be found among the humble people.

A. W. Tozer

Faith itself cannot be strong where humility is weak.

C. H. Spurgeon

One never can see, or not till long afterwards, why any one was selected for any job. And when one does, it is usually some reason that leaves no room for vanity.

C. S. Lewis

All kindness and good deeds, we must keep silent. The result will be an inner reservoir of personality power.

Catherine Marshall

*Finally, all of you should be
of one mind, full of sympathy
toward each other,
loving one another with
tender hearts and humble minds.*

—

1 Peter 3:8 NLT

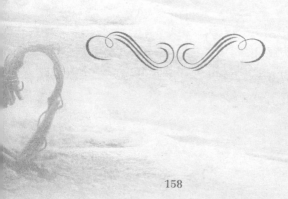

Therefore humble yourselves under the mighty hand of God, that He may exalt you at the proper time, casting all your anxiety on Him, because He cares for you.

1 Peter 5:6-7 NASB

God has chosen you and made you his holy people. He loves you. So always do these things: Show mercy to others, be kind, humble, gentle, and patient.

Colossians 3:12 NCV

Do nothing out of rivalry or conceit, but in humility consider others as more important than yourselves.

Philippians 2:3 HCSB

Let another praise you, and not your own mouth—a stranger, and not your own lips.

Proverbs 27:2 HCSB

Praise the Lord, all nations! Glorify Him, all peoples! For great is His faithful love to us; the Lord's faithfulness endures forever. Hallelujah!

Psalm 117:1-2 HCSB

Jesus had a humble heart.
If He abides in us,
pride will never
dominate our lives.

—

Billy Graham

Chapter 20

What Kind of Example?

*You should be an example to the believers
in speech, in conduct, in love, in faith, in purity.*

—

1 Timothy 4:12 HCSB

Whether we like it or not, all of us are role models. Our friends and family members watch our actions and, as followers of Christ, we are obliged to act accordingly.

What kind of example are you? Are you the kind of person whose life serves as a genuine example of righteousness? Are you a person whose behavior serves as a positive role model for young people? Are you the kind of person whose actions, day in and day out, are based upon kindness, faithfulness, and a love for the Lord? If so, you are not only blessed by God, you are also a powerful force for good in a world that desperately needs positive influences such as yours.

Corrie ten Boom advised, "Don't worry about what you do not understand. Worry about what you do understand in the Bible but do not live by." And that's sound advice because our families and friends are watching . . . and so, for that matter, is God.

You can never separate a leader's actions from his character.

John Maxwell

Let us preach you, Dear Jesus, without preaching, not by words but by our example, by the casting force, the sympathetic influence of what we do, the evident fullness of the love our hearts bear to you. Amen.

Mother Teresa

Your life is destined to be an example. The only question is "what kind?"

Marie T. Freeman

The religion of Jesus Christ has an ethical as well as a doctrinal side.

Lottie Moon

Integrity of heart is indispensable.

John Calvin

If I take care of my character, my reputation will take care of itself.

D. L. Moody

There is no way to grow a saint overnight. Character, like the oak tree, does not spring up like a mushroom.

Vance Havner

Character is both developed and revealed by tests, and all of life is a test.

Rick Warren

In serving we uncover the greatest fulfillment within and become a stellar example of a woman who knows and loves Jesus.

Vonette Bright

We are to leave an impression on all those we meet that communicates whose we are and what kingdom we represent.

Lisa Bevere

Maintaining your integrity
in a world of sham
is no small accomplishment.

—

Wayne Oates

We have around us many people whose lives tell us what faith means. So let us run the race that is before us and never give up. We should remove from our lives anything that would get in the way and the sin that so easily holds us back.

Hebrews 12:1 NCV

In every way be an example of doing good deeds. When you teach, do it with honesty and seriousness.

Titus 2:7 NCV

In everything you do, stay away from complaining and arguing, so that no one can speak a word of blame against you. You are to live clean, innocent lives as children of God in a dark world full of crooked and perverse people. Let your lives shine brightly before them.

Philippians 2:14-15 NLT

For the kingdom of God is not in talk but in power.

1 Corinthians 4:20 HCSB

You are the light that gives light to the world. In the same way, you should be a light for other people. Live so that they will see the good things you do and will praise your Father in heaven.

Matthew 5:14,16 NCV

Don't be deceived: God is not mocked. For whatever a man sows he will also reap, because the one who sows to his flesh will reap corruption from the flesh, but the one who sows to the Spirit will reap eternal life from the Spirit.

Galatians 6:7-8 HCSB

Therefore, get your minds ready for action, being self-disciplined, and set your hope completely on the grace to be brought to you at the revelation of Jesus Christ. As obedient children, do not be conformed to the desires of your former ignorance but, as the One who called you is holy, you also are to be holy in all your conduct.

1 Peter 1:13-15 HCSB

There is nothing anybody else
can do that can stop
God from using us.
We can turn everything
into a testimony.

—

Corrie ten Boom

Chapter 21

Critics Beware

*Don't speak evil against each other,
my dear brothers and sisters. If you criticize each
other and condemn each other, then you are
criticizing and condemning God's law.
But you are not a judge who can decide whether
the law is right or wrong. Your job is to obey it.*

—

James 4:11 NLT

From experience, we know that it is easier to criticize than to correct. And we know that it is easier to find faults than solutions. Yet the urge to criticize others remains a powerful temptation for most of us.

In chapter 4 verse 11, James issues a clear warning against criticizing others. Undoubtedly, James understood the paralyzing power of chronic negativity, and so should we. Our task, as obedient believers, is to break the twin habits of negative thinking and critical speech.

Negativity is highly contagious: we give it to others who, in turn, give it back to us. This cycle can be broken by positive thoughts, heartfelt prayers, and encouraging words. As thoughtful servants of a loving God, we can use the transforming power of Christ's love to break the chains of negativity. And we should.

Being critical of others, including God, is one way we try to avoid facing and judging our own sins.

Warren Wiersbe

If I long to improve my brother, the first step toward doing so is to improve myself.

Christina Rossetti

It takes less sense to criticize than to do anything else. There are a great many critics in the asylum.

Sam Jones

Do not think of the faults of others but of what is good in them and faulty in yourself.

St. Teresa of Avila

Jesus draws near to those who are afflicted and persecuted and criticized and ostracized.

Anne Graham Lotz

Discouraged people don't need critics. They hurt enough already. They don't need more guilt or piled-on distress. They need encouragement. They need a refuge, a willing, caring, available someone.

Charles Swindoll

Discouraged people, if they must be discouraged, ought, at least, to keep their discouragements to themselves, hidden away in the privacy of their own bosoms lest they should discourage the hearts of their brethren.

Hannah Whitall Smith

The scrutiny we give other people should be for ourselves.

Oswald Chambers

After one hour in heaven, we shall be ashamed that we ever grumbled.

Vance Havner

172

A pessimist is someone who
believes that when
her cup runneth over
she'll need a mop.

—

Barbara Johnson

Our Father is kind; you be kind. Don't pick on people, jump on their failures, criticize their faults— unless, of course, you want the same treatment. Don't condemn those who are down; that hardness can boomerang. Be easy on people; you'll find life a lot easier.

Luke 6:36-37 MSG

A man who lacks judgment derides his neighbor, but a man of understanding holds his tongue.

Proverbs 11:12 NIV

So let's agree to use all our energy in getting along with each other. Help others with encouraging words; don't drag them down by finding fault.

Romans 14:19-20 MSG

So in everything, do to others what you would have them do to you, for this sums up the Law and the Prophets.

Matthew 7:12 NIV

Those people are on a dark spiral downward. But if you think that leaves you on the high ground where you can point your finger at others, think again. Every time you criticize someone, you condemn yourself. It takes one to know one. Judgmental criticism of others is a well-known way of escaping detection in your own crimes and misdemeanors. But God isn't so easily diverted. He sees right through all such smoke screens and holds you to what you've done.

Romans 2:1-2 MSG

All bitterness, anger and wrath, insult and slander must be removed from you, along with all wickedness. And be kind and compassionate to one another, forgiving one another, just as God also forgave you in Christ.

Ephesians 4:31-32 HCSB

Be hospitable to one another without complaining.

1 Peter 4:9 HCSB

Our Lord worked with
people as they were,
and He was patient—
not tolerant of sin,
but compassionate.

—

Vance Havner

Chapter 22

The Power of Optimism

But if we look forward to something
we don't have yet,
we must wait patiently and confidently.

—

Romans 8:25 NLT

Are you a hope-filled, enthusiastic Christian? You should be. After all, as a believer, you have every reason to be optimistic about your life here on earth and your eternal life in heaven. As English clergyman William Ralph Inge observed, "No Christian should be a pessimist, for Christianity is a system of radical optimism." Inge's words are most certainly true, but sometimes, you may find yourself pulled down by the inevitable concerns of everyday life. If you find yourself discouraged, exhausted, or both, then it's time to ask yourself this question: what's bothering you, and why?

If you're overly worried by the inevitable ups and downs of life, God wants to have a little chat with you. After all, God has made promises to you that He intends to keep. And if your life has been transformed by God's only begotten Son, then you, as a recipient of God's grace, have every reason to live courageously.

Are you willing to trust God's plans for your life? Hopefully, you will trust Him completely. After all, the words of the psalmist make it clear: "The ways of God are without fault. The Lord's words are pure. He is a shield to those who trust him" (Psalm 18:30 NCV). These words should serve as a reminder that even when the challenges of the day seem daunting, God remains steadfast. And, so should you.

So make this promise to yourself and keep it—vow to be an expectant, faith-filled Christian. Think optimistically about your life, your profession, your family, your future, and your purpose for living. Trust your hopes and not your fears. Take time to celebrate God's glorious creation. And then, when you've filled your heart with hope and gladness, share your optimism with your loved ones. They'll be better for it, and so will you.

Christ can put a spring in your step and a thrill in your heart. Optimism and cheerfulness are products of knowing Christ.

—

Billy Graham

The popular idea of faith is of a certain obstinate optimism: the hope, tenaciously held in the face of trouble, that the universe is fundamentally friendly and things may get better.

J. I. Packer

We may run, walk, stumble, drive, or fly, but let us never lose sight of the reason for the journey, or miss a chance to see a rainbow on the way.

Gloria Gaither

Hope looks for the good in people, opens doors for people, discovers what can be done to help, lights a candle, does not yield to cynicism. Hope sets people free.

Barbara Johnson

The Christian lifestyle is not one of legalistic do's and don'ts, but one that is positive, attractive, and joyful.

Vonette Bright

It is a remarkable thing that some of the most optimistic and enthusiastic people you will meet are those who have been through intense suffering.

Warren Wiersbe

Keep your feet on the ground, but let your heart soar as high as it will. Refuse to be average or to surrender to the chill of your spiritual environment.

A. W. Tozer

If our hearts have been attuned to God through an abiding faith in Christ, the result will be joyous optimism and good cheer.

Billy Graham

Make the least of all that goes and the most of all that comes. Don't regret what is past. Cherish what you have. Look forward to all that is to come. And most important of all, rely moment by moment on Jesus Christ.

Gigi Graham Tchividjian

Make me hear joy and gladness.

Psalm 51:8 NKJV

My cup runs over. Surely goodness and mercy shall follow me all the days of my life; and I will dwell in the house of the Lord forever.

Psalm 23:5-6 NKJV

I can do everything through him that gives me strength.

Philippians 4:13 NIV

For God has not given us a spirit of fear, but of power and of love and of a sound mind.

2 Timothy 1:7 NLT

Be of good courage, and he shall strengthen your heart, all ye that hope in the LORD.

Psalm 31:24 KJV

*The Lord is my light and
my salvation; whom shall I fear?
The Lord is the strength of my life;
of whom shall I be afraid?*

—

Psalm 27:1 KJV

183

The people whom I have seen
succeed best in life have
always been cheerful and
hopeful people who went
about their business with
a smile on their faces.

—

Charles Kingsley

Chapter 23

The Importance of Words

*So then, rid yourselves of all evil, all lying,
hypocrisy, jealousy, and evil speech.
As newborn babies want milk,
you should want the pure and simple teaching.
By it you can grow up and be saved.*

—

1 Peter 2:1–2 NCV

As you think about the day ahead, think about the quality and tone of the words you intend to speak. Hopefully, you understand that your words have great power . . . because they most certainly do. If your words are encouraging, you can lift others up; if your words are hurtful, you can hold others back.

The Bible makes it clear that "Careless words stab like a sword." So, if you hope to solve problems instead of starting them, you must measure your words carefully. But sometimes, you'll be tempted to speak first and think second (with decidedly mixed results).

When you're frustrated or tired, you may say things that would be better left unspoken. Whenever you lash out in anger, you forgo the wonderful opportunity to consider your thoughts before you give voice to them. When you speak impulsively, you may, quite unintentionally, injure others.

A far better strategy, of course, is to do the more difficult thing: to think first and to speak next. When you do so, you give yourself ample time to compose your thoughts and to consult our Creator (but not necessarily in that order!).

Do you seek to be a continuing source of encouragement to others? Do you want to be a beacon of hope to your friends and family? And, do you seek to be a worthy ambassador for Christ? If so, you must speak words that are worthy of your Savior. So avoid angry outbursts. Refrain from impulsive outpourings. Terminate tantrums. Instead, speak words of encouragement and hope to a world that desperately needs both.

Change the heart,
and you change the speech.

—

Warren Wiersbe

What are God's servants but His minstrels, who must inspire the hearts of men and stir them to spiritual joy!

St. Francis of Assisi

Every word we speak, every action we take, has an effect on the totality of humanity. No one can escape that privilege—or that responsibility.

Laurie Beth Jones

The things that we feel most deeply we ought to learn to be silent about, at least until we have talked them over thoroughly with God.

Elisabeth Elliot

Fill the heart with the love of Christ so that only truth and purity can come out of the mouth.

Warren Wiersbe

A little kindly advice is better than a great deal of scolding.

Fanny Crosby

The battle of the tongue is won not in the mouth, but in the heart.

Annie Chapman

Like dynamite, God's power is only latent power until it is released. You can release God's dynamite power into people's lives and the world through faith, your words, and prayer.

Bill Bright

Happy the man whose words issue from the Holy Spirit and not from himself.

Anthony of Padua

We can never love our neighbor too much.

St. Francis of Sales

Be gracious in your speech. The goal is to bring out the best in others in a conversation, not put them down, not cut them out.

Colossians 4:6 MSG

To everything there is a season . . . a time to keep silence, and a time to speak.

Ecclesiastes 3:1, 7 KJV

Watch the way you talk. Let nothing foul or dirty come out of your mouth. Say only what helps, each word a gift.

Ephesians 4:29 MSG

If anyone considers himself religious and yet does not keep a tight rein on his tongue, he deceives himself and his religion is worthless.

James 1:26 NIV

Patience is better than strength.

Proverbs 16:32 ICB

*Patience and encouragement
come from God.
And I pray that God
will help you all agree with
each other the way
Christ Jesus wants.*

—

Romans 15:5 NCV

In all your deeds and words,
you should look on Jesus
as your model,
whether you are keeping
silence or speaking,
whether you are alone
or with others.

—

St. Bonaventure

Chapter 24

Cheerful Christianity

Be cheerful. Keep things in good repair.
Keep your spirits up. Think in harmony.
Be agreeable. Do all that, and the God of love
and peace will be with you for sure.

—

2 Corinthians 13:11 MSG

Cheerfulness is a gift that we give to others and to ourselves. And, as believers who have been saved by a risen Christ, why shouldn't we be cheerful? The answer, of course, is that we have every reason to honor our Savior with joy in our hearts, smiles on our faces, and words of celebration on our lips.

Few things in life are more sad, or, for that matter, more absurd, than the sight of grumpy Christians trudging unhappily through life. Christ promises us lives of abundance and joy if we accept His love and His grace. Yet sometimes, even the most righteous among us are beset by fits of ill temper and frustration. During these moments, we may not feel like turning our thoughts and prayers to Christ, but that's precisely what we should do.

Mrs. Charles E. Cowman, the author of the classic devotional text *Streams in the Desert*, wrote, "Two wings are necessary to lift our souls toward God: prayer and praise. Prayer asks. Praise accepts the answer." That's why we should find the time to lift our concerns to

God in prayer, and to praise Him for all that He has done.

John Wesley correctly observed, "Sour godliness is the devil's religion." These words remind us that pessimism and doubt are some of the most important tools that Satan uses to achieve his objectives. Our challenge, of course, is to ensure that Satan cannot use these tools on us.

Are you a cheerful Christian? You should be! And what is the best way to attain the joy that is rightfully yours? By giving Christ what is rightfully His: your heart, your soul, and your life.

Hope is the power of being cheerful in circumstances which we know to be desperate.

—

G. K. Chesterton

The Bible instructs—and experience teaches—that praising God results in our burdens being lifted and our joys being multiplied.

Jim Gallery

The greatest honor you can give Almighty God is to live gladly and joyfully because of the knowledge of His love.

Juliana of Norwich

God is good, and heaven is forever. And if those two facts don't cheer you up, nothing will.

Marie T. Freeman

We may run, walk, stumble, drive, or fly, but let us never lose sight of the reason for the journey, or miss a chance to see a rainbow on the way.

Gloria Gaither

When we bring sunshine into the lives of others, we're warmed by it ourselves. When we spill a little happiness, it splashes on us.

Barbara Johnson

Make each day useful and cheerful and prove that you know the worth of time by employing it well. Then youth will be happy, old age without regret, and life a beautiful success.

Louisa May Alcott

Be assured, my dear friend, that it is no joy to God in seeing you with a dreary countenance.

C. H. Spurgeon

Joy in life is not the absence of sorrow. The fact that Jesus could have joy in the midst of sorrow is proof that we can experience this too.

Warren Wiersbe

God loves a cheerful giver.

2 Corinthians 9:7 NIV

Rejoice in the Lord always. I will say it again: Rejoice!

Philippians 4:4 HCSB

Do everything readily and cheerfully—no bickering, no second-guessing allowed! Go out into the world uncorrupted, a breath of fresh air in this squalid and polluted society. Provide people with a glimpse of good living and of the living God. Carry the light-giving Message into the night.

Philippians 2:14-15 MSG

Is anyone happy? Let him sing songs of praise

James 5:13 NIV

A cheerful look brings joy to the heart, and good news gives health to the bones.

Proverbs 15:30 NIV

198

Jacob said, "For what a relief it is
to see your friendly smile.
It is like seeing the smile of God!"

—

Genesis 33:10 NLT

A life of intimacy with God
is characterized by joy.

—

Oswald Chambers

Chapter 25

Following Christ

*Then He said to them all,
"If anyone wants to come with Me,
he must deny himself, take up his cross daily,
and follow Me."*

—

Luke 9:23 HCSB

Jesus walks with you. Are you walking with Him? Hopefully, you will choose to walk with Him today and every day of your life. Jesus loved you so much that He endured unspeakable humiliation and suffering for you. How will you respond to Christ's sacrifice? Will you take up His cross and follow Him (Luke 9:23), or will you choose another path? When you place your hopes squarely at the foot of the cross, when you place Jesus squarely at the center of your life, you will be blessed. If you seek to be a worthy disciple of Jesus, you must acknowledge that He never comes "next." He is always first.

Do you hope to fulfill God's purpose for your life? Do you seek a life of abundance and peace? Do you intend to be Christian, not just in name, but in deed? Then follow Christ. Follow Him by picking up His cross today and every day that you live. When you do, you will quickly discover that Christ's love has the power to change everything, including you.

Jesus makes God visible. But that truth does not make Him somehow less than God. He is equally supreme with God.

Anne Graham Lotz

Jesus was the perfect reflection of God's nature in every situation He encountered during His time here on earth.

Bill Hybels

Had Jesus been the Word become word, He would have spun theories about life, but since He was the Word become flesh, He put shoes on all His theories and made them walk.

E. Stanley Jones

Christians see sin for what it is: willful rebellion against the rulership of God in their lives. And in turning from their sin, they have embraced God's only means of dealing with sin: Jesus.

Kay Arthur

Tell me the story of Jesus. Write on my heart every word. Tell me the story most precious, sweetest that ever was heard.

Fanny Crosby

There is not a single thing that Jesus cannot change, control, and conquer because He is the living Lord.

Franklin Graham

The crucial question for each of us is this: What do you think of Jesus, and do you yet have a personal acquaintance with Him?

Hannah Whitall Smith

In your greatest weakness, turn to your greatest strength, Jesus, and hear Him say, "My grace is sufficient for you, for My strength is made perfect in weakness" (2 Corinthians 12:9 NKJV).

Lisa Whelchel

Sold for thirty pieces of silver, he redeemed the world.

R. G. Lee

The Word had become flesh, a real human baby. He had not ceased to be God. He was no less God than before, but He had begun to be man. He was not now God minus some elements of His deity but God plus all that He had made His own by taking manhood to himself.

J. I. Packer

I am truly happy with Jesus Christ. I couldn't live without Him. When my life gets beyond the ability to cope, He takes over.

Ruth Bell Graham

When you can't see him, trust him. Jesus is closer than you ever dreamed.

Max Lucado

Love consists in this: not that we loved God, but that He loved us and sent His Son to be the propitiation for our sins.

1 John 4:10 HCSB

Therefore if any man be in Christ, he is a new creature: old things are passed away; behold, all things are become new.

2 Corinthians 5:17 KJV

In the beginning was the Word, and the Word was with God, and the Word was God. . . . And the Word was made flesh, and dwelt among us, (and we beheld his glory, the glory as of the only begotten of the Father,) full of grace and truth.

John 1:1, 14 KJV

I have come as a light into the world, so that everyone who believes in Me would not remain in darkness.

John 12:46 HCSB

The next day John saw Jesus coming toward him and said, "Here is the Lamb of God, who takes away the sin of the world!"

John 1:29 HCSB

But we do see Jesus—made lower than the angels for a short time so that by God's grace He might taste death for everyone—crowned with glory and honor because of the suffering of death.

Hebrews 2:9 HCSB

For unto us a Child is born, unto us a Son is given; and the government will be upon His shoulder. And His name will be called Wonderful, Counselor, Mighty God, Everlasting Father, Prince of Peace.

Isaiah 9:6 NKJV

Jesus Christ is the same yesterday, today, and forever.

Hebrews 13:8 HCSB

The only source of Life
is the Lord Jesus Christ.

—

Oswald Chambers